THE WORLD CUP
SOCCER'S GLOBAL CHAMPIONSHIP

Matt Doeden

MILLBROOK PRESS · MINNEAPOLIS

Millbrook Press
A division of Lerner Publishing Group, Inc.
241 First Avenue North
Minneapolis, MN 55401 USA

For reading levels and more information, look up this title at www.lernerbooks.com.

Main body text set in Adobe Garamond Pro Regular 14/19.
Typeface provided by Adobe Systems.

Library of Congress Cataloging-in-Publication Data

Names: Doeden, Matt.
Title: The world cup : soccer's global championship / By Matt Doeden.
Description: Minneapolis : Millbrook Press, [2018] | Series: Spectacular sports |
  Includes bibliographical references and index.
Identifiers: LCCN 2017009220 (print) | LCCN 2017014231 (ebook) |
  ISBN 9781512498684 (eb pdf) | ISBN 9781512427554 (lb : alk. paper)
Subjects: LCSH: World Cup (Soccer)—Juvenile literature. | Soccer—Juvenile
  literature.
Classification: LCC GV943.49 (ebook) | LCC GV943.49 .D64 2018 (print) |
  DDC 796.334/66809—dc23

LC record available at https://lccn.loc.gov/2017009220

Manufactured in the United States of America
1-41488-23351-9/7/2017

CONTENTS

INTRODUCTION:
WORLD DOMINANCE

Chants from frenzied fans echo across the packed stadium. Flags and banners wave in the breeze. Camera flashes light up the stands as a midfielder boots a long pass in front of the goal. Dirt flies from underfoot when a forward streaks toward the ball. The goalkeeper dives as the forward unleashes a blazing shot. Victory in the world's biggest soccer tournament is at stake, and it all comes down to this moment.

It's the final match of the World Cup, the crown jewel of international soccer. Since its modest beginnings in 1930, the World Cup has exploded in popularity, creating an international soccer community in a way that no other sport can match. It only happens once every four years, and worldwide bragging rights are on the line.

Mario Götze (*right*) scores a goal for Germany in the 2014 World Cup final match. Germany won the game, 1–0.

This illustration shows a soccer match between England and Scotland in the 1870s. The goal (*left*) had no net and consisted of two poles with a rope running along the top.

1 FROM POLITICS TO PELÉ:

THE ROAD TO THE WORLD CUP

Soccer—or football as it's known to most of the world—was far from an international craze when Scotland and England faced off for the world's first international match in 1872. While club play—matches between organized local teams—had grown wildly popular in Britain, soccer had little foothold outside the British Isles. And so the world wasn't exactly paying attention as 11 English players took to the pitch to take on 11 Scottish opponents. England brought an all-star team handpicked from club teams. Scotland, meanwhile, fielded a team composed entirely of players from a single club, Glasgow's Queen's Park.

A crowd of 4,000 fans turned out at Hamilton Crescent, a muddy, rain-soaked cricket field in Glasgow—most of them to cheer on their fellow Scots. It was a gritty defensive battle between the blue-shirted Scots and the white-clad English. The English were bigger, stronger, and more talented. However, the Scots were used to playing with one another, and their smaller size made them faster than the English, even on the sloppy mud that covered the field.

Scotland pushed the action in the first half, while the English were on the attack for much of the second half. Scotland recorded a pair of near misses. But that's as close as either side came to scoring. And so the first international soccer match ended in a scoreless tie. It may not have seemed like much at the time, but the 0–0 deadlock marked the beginning of a new era in soccer. The sport had stepped onto the world stage, and soccer would never be the same.

FIFA AND THE FIRST WORLD CUP

By 1900 soccer was well on its way to world domination. As the sport spread through Europe and into the Americas, professional associations (leagues) popped up all around the globe. The sport was included as part of the 1900 Olympic Games, with Great Britain beating France in the final match. However, the Olympic teams were composed only of amateur players. Professionals weren't allowed. Since the Olympics didn't include some of the best players in the world, these games didn't really address the question of soccer superiority. Yet the event did raise public interest in a true international competition. Two years later, Argentina routed Uruguay, 6–0, in the first international match ever held outside the British Isles.

Even though the game was spreading, Europe remained the center of the soccer world. By 1904 Europe's many associations needed a common governing body to oversee international competition. That year several European nations formed the Fédération Internationale de Football Association (FIFA). FIFA's grip on the game grew quickly. It oversaw the soccer competition at the 1908 Olympics. It expanded to South Africa in 1909 and Argentina in 1912. FIFA was fast becoming the dominant governing force in the ever-expanding international game.

The seeds of the World Cup were sown in 1908 when Turin, Italy, hosted the Torneo Internazionale Stampa Sportiva. Unlike the Olympic Games, this tournament included top professionals from around the globe. The event featured

Great Britain (*in white with black shorts*) beat Denmark, 2–0, for the gold medal at the 1908 Olympics in London, England.

an international group of association teams, rather than national teams composed of a country's top players, which fans would later see in World Cup tournaments. But the matches in Turin gathered the world's best players together in a series of nation vs. nation clashes.

Soccer took a back seat in Europe as World War I (1914–1918) raged through the continent, and the game was slow to recover there. As Europe endured war and its aftermath, the balance of soccer power began to shift to South America. Uruguay won gold at both the 1924 and 1928 Olympics. Its hopes at a third straight title were dashed, however, when soccer wasn't even included at the 1932 games in Los Angeles, California. The sport was dropped in part because FIFA wanted to use pro players, while the Olympic committee did not, and also because the sport's popularity in the United States, the host country for the 1932 games, lagged far behind much of the rest of the world.

FIFA president Jules Rimet believed the sport was in need of something big to reach its full potential. So he introduced an idea for a new international tournament. It would feature national teams made up of a country's top players—but unlike the Olympics, this tournament would feature professional players. The World Cup, he proposed, would be held every four years to decide which nation truly ruled the international game. FIFA announced that Uruguay would host the first World Cup in 1930.

It was an ambitious plan. The 1930 tournament, however, fell flat. An economic crisis called the Great Depression (1929–1942) had gripped the world. For European nations, a trip to South America would be costly. Many simply declined the invitation. That included England, which would have been the overwhelming favorite to win the title.

Lucien Laurent (*front row, center*) is shown with some of his French teammates. He died in 2005 about four months after his 97th birthday.

The 1930 World Cup had 13 teams. Seven came from South American nations. Two were from North America. Just four were from Europe. The first matches were played on July 13.

Lucien Laurent of France scored the first World Cup goal. He later said that no one at the time could have guessed how big the World Cup would one day become. "We were playing Mexico and it was snowing, since it was winter in the southern hemisphere," Laurent said. "One of my teammates centered the ball and I followed its path carefully, taking it on the volley with my right foot [and scoring a goal]. Everyone was pleased but we didn't all roll around on the ground. Nobody realized that history was being made. A quick handshake and we got on with the game."

Despite the lack of participation from England and other important soccer nations, the first World Cup succeeded in igniting the passion of certain soccer fans, especially in South America. The final came down to two South American countries, Uruguay and Argentina. Fans from Argentina flocked to Uruguay for the July 30 final. However, they left disappointed. Uruguay thrilled the home crowd with a 4–2 victory to become the first world champion and claim the Coupe du Monde (which later became known as the Jules Rimet Cup, or the Jules Rimet Trophy). The nation declared a national holiday to celebrate. Meanwhile, heartbroken Argentina fans back home in Buenos Aires responded by throwing stones at Uruguay's consulate.

Uruguay scores a goal during the 1930 World Cup. They won the tournament that year and again in 1950.

TROUBLED TIMES

The 1934 World Cup was held in Italy. Uruguay, bitter that most of Europe had declined to make the trip to South America four years earlier, boycotted, refusing to defend their title. Italy and Czechoslovakia met in the final match. After a scoreless first half, Czechoslovakia scored in the 71st minute. The Italian fans grew nervous as the minutes ticked away. But Italy tied the score 10 minutes later and then won the World Cup title on a goal by Angelo Schiavio in extra time.

Bitterness between soccer powers in South America and Europe carried into the 1938 tournament. Several South American teams boycotted the games, this time held in France. Yet much more ominous political problems were on the horizon. Europe was swept up in a rapidly escalating crisis as the Nazi Party that controlled Germany grew more and more aggressive, and the specter of war hung over the continent. Against this uneasy backdrop, Italy defended its title, becoming the first nonhost nation to claim the trophy.

Czechoslovakia's goalkeeper bats the ball away from his goal during the 1934 World Cup.

THE FORMAT

For every World Cup but the 1950 tournament, FIFA has stuck to the same basic formula. The tournament plays out in two phases, or stages. The group stage comes first. The teams are divided into groups of four teams each, and a team plays every other team in its group.

The top two teams from each group advance to the second phase. The tournament stage, or knockout round, is a single-elimination tournament. The teams fight it out until only two remain. They battle in the championship match for World Cup glory.

International soccer halted during World War II (1939–1945) as fighting took place across Europe, northern Africa, and Asia. Meanwhile, Ottorino Barassi, the Italian vice president of FIFA, feared that the Nazis would steal the valuable Coupe du Monde. Barassi hid the trophy in a shoe box under his bed. That's where it stayed as the war raged, waiting for the world's biggest soccer tournament to resume.

A NEW ERA

World War II had taken a heavy toll, especially in Europe. The continent was focused on rebuilding and healing. The scars of war were simply too fresh for FIFA to hold the tournament. For the second straight time, the event was canceled.

Brazil was determined to bring the tournament back in a big way. In 1950 the World Cup returned to South America for the first time in 20 years. Brazil built the world's largest soccer stadium, Maracanã, to host the event. The Brazilians were wild about the sport, and their team was widely expected to dominate in front of the home crowds.

THE STRANGE SAGA OF THE JULES RIMET TROPHY

The history of the Jules Rimet Trophy is filled with mystery. The trophy, originally called the Coupe du Monde, stood 15 inches (37 cm) high. It featured Nike, the Greek goddess of victory. Italy won the cup in 1938, just before World War II broke out. The trophy spent the war hidden in a shoe box under the bed of Ottorino Barassi, the Italian vice president of FIFA.

West Germany claimed the Rimet Trophy in 1954. But when the prize returned for the 1958 World Cup in Sweden, it looked quite different. The trophy was taller, with a bigger base. No one could—or was willing to—explain it. Many believe it was a replica. The original may have been lost or stolen.

Months before the 1966 World Cup in England, the trophy was stolen. As FIFA officials scrambled to replace it, they received the lid to the cup in the mail and a ransom note.

The search for the stolen cup dragged on for a week. David Corbett was not part of the search. But one week after the theft, Corbett was walking his dog, Pickles, in a suburb south of London. The dog began sniffing under a bush. There, Corbett discovered the Rimet Trophy, wrapped in newspaper. Pickles received a handsome reward—a year's supply of dog food—and became an international canine celebrity.

When he started the World Cup, Rimet said that the first nation to win three World Cups would be allowed to keep the trophy. In 1970 Brazil completed that feat. A new trophy was made (*left*), as the original remained locked away in a Rio de Janeiro trophy case—behind bulletproof glass—until 1983. Then, once again, it was stolen. This time, the trophy was never found. Officials believe it was melted down for its precious metals.

The 1950 World Cup marked the start of a new era. The petty prewar political bickering between Europe and South America was long gone. For the first time, England took part in the event. Their debut didn't go as expected, however. The nation that invented the game lost to the United States, where soccer was largely an afterthought.

England's loss was a shocker. But the big shock was yet to come. As expected, Brazil rolled to the final game. They faced Uruguay for the World Cup crown in front of 200,000 rabid fans—most supporting the home team. Brazil took a 1–0 advantage early in the second half. But Uruguay stunned the crowd with two late goals and one of the biggest upsets in World Cup history.

It hadn't gone the way Brazil's fans had wanted. But one thing was certain. The World Cup was back in a big way.

SUPERSTARS AND DYNASTIES

The World Cup was growing into one of the world's major sporting events. It was televised for the first time in 1954, when the tournament was held in Switzerland. Television viewers were treated to an offensive spectacle. Hungary fielded a team filled with dizzying offensive talent, led by its star, Ferenc "Galloping Major" Puskás. The Hungarians scored a stunning 17 goals in their first two games alone. Yet they couldn't finish the job, losing to West Germany in a match known as the Miracle of Berne.

Puskás, a flashy goal-scoring machine, was the sort of superstar that fans loved. But he would soon be overshadowed by another soccer sensation. The 1958 World Cup, held in Sweden, saw the international debut of a new, rising talent from Brazil. A slim 17-year-old named Edson Arantes do Nascimento—better known as Pelé—burst onto the scene. Pelé was ready to take the sport to a new level of popularity. He netted the game-winning goal against Wales, scored a hat trick against France, and then added two more goals in Brazil's 5–2 victory over Sweden in the championship match. Pelé had been just nine years old when Brazil lost to Uruguay in 1950. Yet his play in 1958 finally helped Brazilian fans forget the pain of the team's earlier loss. Brazil's title also marked the first time that a team from outside the host continent won the Jules Rimet Trophy.

Pelé's stunning performance marked the start of a new era in soccer. The sport had always had its stars. But none could compare to the fleet-footed young Brazilian. Brazil became the world power in soccer, but Pelé didn't do it alone. The country won the World Cup again in 1962, despite losing its young star to injury in the second game.

Pelé returned to the World Cup stage in 1966 in England. But the games against Bulgaria and Portugal didn't go well. The Bulgarians violently fouled Pelé again and again. Portugal used the same strategy two games later. At the time, the World Cup did not allow teams to substitute players. Pelé was forced to keep playing, limping and ineffective, as Brazil was knocked out of the tournament. The intentionally rough treatment of the game's biggest star was the story of the tournament—even overshadowing England winning the World Cup in front of its home fans.

Pelé takes a shot during the World Cup in 1958. In 2000 FIFA named Pelé and Argentina's Diego Maradona as the two best players of the 20th century.

Pelé (*in yellow*) scored more than 1,200 goals in fewer than 1,400 career games.

Pelé vowed after the 1966 debacle that he'd never play in another World Cup. But by 1970, he'd changed his mind. It was a happy decision for Brazil and fans of soccer. The 1970 Brazilian team thrilled fans watching at the stadium and on TV— it was the first World Cup broadcast in color. Many have called the 1970 Brazilians the greatest team in the history of the international game. They capped it off with a 4–1 victory over Italy. Pelé's legacy was secured, and Brazil had left no doubt as to which nation was the center of the soccer world.

RISING AFRICA

The World Cup had the potential to be a truly global affair. Yet for half a century, Europe and South America dominated the tournament. By the 1980s, the vision of a competition that spanned the globe started to become a reality.

Africa had long been an afterthought in the international soccer scene. Egypt competed at the 1934 event but didn't win a match. Zaire made the tournament in 1974 but lost the three matches they played by a combined score of 14–0.

In 1978 Tunisia became the first African team to win a match at the World Cup. Four years later, Algeria and Cameroon both competed. But neither advanced out of the tournament's first round, known as the group stage. Algeria was eliminated because of complex tiebreaker rules after a controversial game known as the Disgrace of Gijón, in which West Germany and Austria appeared to work together to finish with a score that knocked Algeria out of the World Cup. In 1986 Morocco became the first African team to advance to the round of 16, the tournament's second stage, before losing to West Germany.

When Cameroon (*in green*) defeated Argentina in the 1990 World Cup, soccer fans around the world celebrated the stunning upset.

Cameroon was the story of the 1990 World Cup. The team was not highly regarded entering the tournament. But that changed when they defeated the defending champions, Argentina, in their opening match. Cameroon's rise was as unlikely as the star who powered it. Roger Milla, a 38-year-old forward, had come out of retirement for the tournament. By international soccer standards, Milla was practically ancient. But he electrified fans and teammates with goal after goal—each followed by a wild celebration. Cameroon advanced to the quarterfinals before being eliminated by England. Their success helped pave the way for more African teams.

WOMEN TAKE THE STAGE

For decades, men's soccer had dominated the international scene. But the popularity of women's soccer was on the rise. In 1988 FIFA was ready to experiment with an international tournament for women. So 12 teams traveled to China for the Women's World Championship, which Norway won.

FIFA considered the tournament a success. In 1991 the organization gave the green light to another competition—also in China. It was the first Women's World Cup. Norway and the United States met in the championship match. The score remained deadlocked at 1–1 until just two minutes were left in the game. That's when US forward Michelle Akers-Stahl stole a pass and buried the game-winner in the back of the Norway goal.

The United States hoisted the World Cup trophy. But the entire women's soccer movement came out victorious. "People around the world have gotten a glimpse of women's football," said FIFA spokesperson Andreas Herren. "They can see that it has all the excitement and emotion and joy the men's game has."

Michelle Akers-Stahl (*in blue*) scored 10 goals for the United States during the 1991 Women's World Cup.

The Women's World Cup only got bigger. In the 1999 final match, a crowd of more than 90,000 fans cheered as the United States defeated China at the Rose Bowl in Pasadena, California. It was the largest crowd ever gathered for a women's sporting event.

The Women's World Cup has continued to grow. Its popularity globally—along with that of women's soccer at the Olympic Games—still lags behind the men's game. Generally, the top women are not paid at the same level as the men, an issue that has led to resentment and lawsuits in recent years. However, in nations such as the United States, Japan, and China, the women's game has flourished. More women are playing—and watching—soccer than ever before.

Team USA celebrates their victory in the final match of the 1999 Women's World Cup. It was the second Women's World Cup title for the United States.

SCANDAL

In 2015 FIFA was rocked by scandal. On May 27, Swiss law enforcement agents descended on the Baur au Lac, a luxury hotel in Zurich, Switzerland, the site of FIFA's annual meeting. The officers arrested seven of FIFA's top officials on charges of corruption that stretched back decades. More arrests were made in the following months.

The news stunned the international soccer world. The FIFA officials were accused of taking massive bribes and buying and selling votes that determine, among other things, where major tournaments take place. Among the accusations was that officials took a $10 million bribe to name South Africa as the 2010 World Cup site. Evidence pointed to huge payoffs and to an organizational structure that was corrupt from the top down.

The arrests were international news. Yet the annual meeting went on. Just two days after the arrests, FIFA voted to reelect Sepp Blatter (*right*) to another four-year term as president. Blatter, while not among those arrested, was already a controversial figure. His reelection drew worldwide criticism and calls for FIFA to reform. Blatter resigned a year later under mounting pressure to step down. Meanwhile, FIFA suspended the awarding of the 2026 World Cup to a host city.

CONTINUED EXPANSION

Over the decades, as both the men's and women's versions of the World Cup have grown, more and more nations have fielded teams. In 1982 the tournament expanded from 16 to 24 teams. Then, in 1998, it grew to the current size of 32 teams.

Meanwhile, the qualification process for both the men's and women's tournaments has grown increasingly complex, especially for the men. The World Cup plans to expand to 48 teams by 2026. A spot is always reserved for the host nation. Another spot had been set aside for the defending champion. However, that automatic bid disappeared in 2006 when FIFA determined that it was actually

People who are able to attend World Cup matches represent just a tiny portion of the total fan base. Millions more people around the world watch on TV and the Internet.

a disadvantage for the team. The defending champions entered the tournament without having played in the competitive qualifying matches, leaving them rusty and more likely to lose. FIFA allocates the rest of the spots by geographic region, weighted toward the game's hot spots (Europe and South America). Teams within each region battle to qualify for the World Cup through a series of tournaments.

The popularity of both tournaments has never been greater. In 2014 more than 3.3 million fans attended World Cup games in Brazil, where Germany defeated Argentina to take the crown. A year later, more than 1.3 million fans attended the Women's World Cup in Canada. The United States defeated Japan to become the first team to claim three Women's World Cups. More than 760 million people tuned in to watch at least part of the final game on TV. That made the match the second most viewed FIFA event in the world (only the men's World Cup drew more viewers). The record viewership showed how much the women's game has grown in only a few decades and hinted at the potential for greater growth.

2 HEROICS AND HEARTBREAK:
MEMORABLE MATCHES AND MOMENTS OF THE WORLD CUP

For nearly a century, the World Cup has provided fans with amazing comebacks, nail-biters, and more than its share of shocking moments—both good and bad. Read on to learn more about the matches and players that have made the World Cup and the Women's World Cup two of the sporting world's biggest international events.

THE FATEFUL FINAL
JULY 16, 1950 • URUGUAY 2, BRAZIL 1

Brazil was all-in for the 1950 World Cup. The host nation and odds-on favorite to win the tournament poured enormous resources into the event. That included the building of the world's largest soccer stadium, the 200,000-seat Maracanã. It marked the World Cup's first return to South America since the tournament in 1930, and the fans were ready for a party.

The Brazilian national team (*in white*) was so heavily favored to win the World Cup that a Brazilian newspaper printed special editions with the headline "Champions of the World" before the start of the final match.

The 1950 World Cup marked a one-time departure from the event's usual setup. Instead of a single-elimination tournament, four finalists took part in a round-robin format, with each team playing the other three. The champion would be the team with the best record in that final round.

On the final day, it came down to Brazil (2–0) versus Uruguay (1–0–1) for the title. Because Brazil had the better record going into the game, they needed only a tie to claim their first World Cup, while Uruguay needed to win.

Fans of Brazil flooded into the stands expecting nothing less than victory. Brazil was by far the stronger team, and the energy of 200,000 rabid fans only seemed to make them better. Brazil came out in their trademark style—relentless attack. But every time they surged, Uruguay pushed back. The first half ended scoreless.

Just two minutes into the second half, the action heated up. Brazil controlled the ball on a rush. Friaça took a low shot, whizzing the ball past the goalkeeper and into the net. The stadium erupted as Brazil celebrated. Uruguay was left arguing with the ref that Brazil had been offside on the play, but their protest was denied. Brazil led, 1–0.

Uruguay regrouped as the deafening roar of the crowd rained down. "Let them shout," said Uruguay's dynamic midfielder Obdulio Varela. "In five minutes the stadium will seem like a graveyard, and then only one voice will be heard. Mine!"

Protecting their lead, Brazil changed tactics. They played back near their goal, adopting a defensive posture. It may have seemed like a good idea. After all, Uruguay needed two goals to take the lead—a tie did them no good. But the change in strategy played right into Uruguay's hands. They pressed the action and took control of the match. In the 66th minute, Varela slid a pass to forward Alcides Ghiggia. Ghiggia sidestepped a defender and streaked down the field. He blasted the ball to the front of the goal, where Juan Alberto Schiaffino knocked it in. The game was tied.

After Alcides Ghiggia's goal to win the 1950 World Cup for Uruguay, the Brazilian team was so upset that they changed the color of their jerseys from white to yellow and green.

The momentum Brazil had built early in the match was gone. Uruguay remained the aggressors, pushing the pace of play and increasing their scoring chances. In the 79th minute, Uruguay's Julio Pérez intercepted a pass and started toward Brazil's end. He exchanged passes with Ghiggia as they crossed midfield, then booted the ball ahead to a teammate. Ghiggia stormed toward the goal, took a pass, and silenced the crowd with a shot that found the corner of the net.

Varela's boast that the stadium would fall silent came true—although it took a bit longer than the five minutes he'd predicted. The Brazilian fans looked on in disbelief as their squad was suddenly behind. Brazil mounted a desperate charge. They forced the ball near the front of the Uruguay goal, but the referee's whistle ended the action before they could get a quality shot. It was over!

The game, nicknamed the Fateful Final, was a humiliating loss for Brazil. Fans around the country took it hard. The Brazilian national team didn't play in their new stadium again for four years. Yet some experts believe that the sting of that loss may have motivated the Brazilian team, pushing them to become the greatest soccer power the international game has ever seen.

THE MIRACLE OF BERN
JULY 4, 1954 • WEST GERMANY 3, HUNGARY 2

The 1950 World Cup had ended in Uruguay's stunning upset of Brazil. Yet an even bigger surprise came four years later. Hungary entered the 1954 tournament as an offensive machine unlike any the world had ever seen. Known as the Golden Team, they hadn't lost an international match in four years. In their first two games of group play, they won by a combined score of 17–3. Led by perhaps the world's greatest player at the time, Ferenc Puskás, they had sliced through the past two champions in Uruguay and Brazil to reach the tournament's final match. Hungary was a team of full-time professionals, and they ran like a well-oiled machine.

West Germany, meanwhile, was playing in just its second World Cup. The nation was still recovering from defeat in World War II. The team was made up of semiprofessional players who earned money playing soccer, but not full time. Their World Cup had gotten off to a rocky start. In one of their games in the group stage, they took an 8–3 drubbing at the hands of Hungary. Yet somehow they qualified for the next round, where they stunned both Yugoslavia and Austria to force a rematch with Hungary for the World Cup crown.

Ferenc Puskás (*left*) blasts a shot against West Germany. He scored 83 goals in the 84 games he played with the Hungarian national team.

West Germany's chances appeared slim as the teams took to the rain-soaked field. The Hungarians swarmed all over the pitch in a style that defied soccer tradition. "Players . . . constantly changed position according to a prearranged plan," Puskás later explained. "Our opponents could not guess our plans and found themselves in difficulties which would not have been experienced had we followed the [traditional style] of play."

West Germany, like so many opponents before them, seemed dumbfounded by the style. Hungary was on fire, scoring two goals in the first eight minutes. The game had all the makings of another blowout.

It wasn't apparent early in the match, but the West Germans had an advantage that day. They were wearing a new type of equipment—shoes with studs that screwed into the bottom, similar to modern-day cleats. As the game went on, the conditions on the wet field grew worse. The Hungarians were slipping and sliding in the slick mud, while the studs gave the West Germans more solid footing. To the amazement of the crowd, the momentum slowly shifted. The West Germans booted home two goals of their own to tie the score, 2–2.

Hungary remained the aggressor in the second half, but West Germany's goalkeeper Toni Turek made save after save. Then, with just six minutes remaining in the match, the West Germans got their chance. They sent a crossing pass to the front of the Hungary goal. The ball was deflected, but it went right to the foot of Helmut Rahn, who slammed it into the bottom corner of the net. The fans looked on in disbelief—as did German play-by-play announcer Herbert Zimmerman. "3–2 to Germany," he shouted in celebration. "Call me mad! Call me crazy!"

With two minutes to play, Puskás appeared to tie the game, but the officials disallowed the goal, calling Hungary offside on the play. It was the last chance the Golden Team would get. The final seconds ticked away, and West Germany walked off with perhaps the greatest upset in World Cup history.

SAVE OF THE CENTURY
JUNE 7, 1970 • BRAZIL 1, ENGLAND 0

Few dispute that Pelé was the greatest player of his era and possibly the best in the history of soccer. But for one moment at the 1970 World Cup, he was upstaged by England's goalkeeper Gordon Banks.

In a scoreless tie in the first half, Brazil forward Jairzinho tracked down the ball deep in the right corner of England's end. Jairzinho zipped a crossing pass directly in front of the goal. Banks, who had been manning the right side of the net, was in deep trouble. That's because the high pass went straight to Pelé on the left side.

Gordon Banks (*left, behind the goalpost*) dives to stop Pelé's header. Brazil won the match, but Banks was already a World Cup champion. He had been England's goalkeeper for the team's World Cup title in 1966.

Pelé leaped high into the air and slammed his head into the ball. His header screamed down and to the left—far from where Banks was scrambling to recover. The England goalkeeper desperately dove for the bouncing ball, deflecting it and sending it over the crossbar.

The crowd roared for a goal. Pelé began to celebrate. Only after a few moments did the truth sink in. Banks had stopped it. It was a save so amazing, so unthinkable, that even the players on the field needed a moment to process it.

"From the moment I headed it, I was sure it had gone in," Pelé said. "After I headed the ball, I had already begun to jump to celebrate the goal. Then I looked back and I couldn't believe it hadn't gone in. I have scored more than a thousand goals in my life and the thing people always talk to me about is the one I didn't score."

In the end, Banks's heroic save wasn't enough. Brazil won the match, 1–0. The Save of the Century lives on, with replays on Internet sites such as YouTube continuing to wow fans almost 50 years later.

GAME OF THE CENTURY

JUNE 17, 1970 • ITALY 4, WEST GERMANY 3

The final match of the 1970 World Cup is known as the Game of the Century, but most of the contest didn't live up to the name. It started as an 89-minute defensive struggle. What followed was a barrage of goals unlike anything the tournament has ever seen.

Italy took a 1–0 lead just eight minutes into the match. For most of the game, it appeared that lone goal would be enough. With both teams playing stifling defense, the score held until the final seconds were ticking away. West Germany was playing with a full team of 11 men, but they were still shorthanded. That's because midfielder Franz Beckenbauer dislocated his shoulder, and West Germany had already used both of their allowed substitutions. Beckenbauer stayed on the pitch, but with his arm in a sling, he could do little more than take up space on the field.

Despite Beckenbauer's injury, West Germany mounted a furious charge in injury time. Karl-Heinz Schnellinger, who was generally not a goal-scoring threat, shocked the Italians by tying the game. The championship match went on to 30 minutes of extra time.

The extra period was an unforgettable, back-and-forth offensive explosion. Gerd Müller started it with a goal for West

Gerd Müller (*left*) smacks a header past Italy's goalkeeper.

Germany in the 94th minute. Italy roared back, tying it again four minutes later, then scoring again to take the lead. In the 110th minute, Müller scored once more to make it 3–3. But as the television broadcast was still showing the replay of Müller's tying goal, Italy's Gianni Rivera took a crossing pass and buried it in the back of the net.

After 90 minutes with just one goal, the teams had combined for six goals in 21 minutes! West Germany wasn't able to answer the fourth Italian goal, and Italy walked off as champions in one of the most heart-stopping finals in World Cup history.

THE DISGRACE OF GIJÓN
JUNE 25, 1982 • WEST GERMANY 1, AUSTRIA 0

Many of the World Cup's most memorable matches featured unexpected or heroic performances. But the tournament also has a darker side. That was never more clear than in a 1982 group match between West Germany and Austria. It's a match that has come to be known as the Disgrace of Gijón.

The teams met in Gijón, Spain, for their final group match. West Germany, Austria, and Algeria were all competing for two spots in the round of 16. Because of a complex tie-breaking system, both West Germany and Austria would advance if West Germany won by a margin of one or two goals. If West Germany lost or tied, they'd be out. If Austria lost by more than two goals, they would be eliminated.

The match started much like any other. West Germany attacked from the opening whistle. Forward Horst Hrubesch found the back of the net, after 10 minutes, to give West Germany a 1–0 lead.

What followed was 80 minutes of the worst play the World Cup has to offer. Both teams appeared to stop trying. They meandered around the field, passing the ball back and forth while making no effort to score. They knew that if the score remained 1–0, both teams would advance. So they simply decided to stop making any effort. As the slow play continued, the crowd grew more and more restless, loudly jeering both sides. Austrian TV commentator Robert Seeger was so disgusted that he told viewers to turn off their sets. German announcer Eberhard Stanjek simply stopped describing the game for TV viewers altogether.

West Germany's coach Jupp Derwall didn't help matters in a postgame interview. "We wanted to [advance in the tournament], not

Fans let a West Germany player know how they feel about the way his team played as he makes his way off the field.

play football," he explained. The next day, a German newspaper ran the headline that read simply, "Shame on you!"

Algerian officials were irate. Clearly, West Germany and Austria had ignored the spirit of the competition to make sure they both advanced. Algeria filed a protest. But because there was no proof of collusion between Austria and West Germany, the protest was dismissed. Algeria was out. Meanwhile, Austria was eliminated in the next round of the tournament, while West Germany advanced to the final match before losing to Italy.

The Disgrace of Gijón wasn't the first or the last time that game-fixing was suspected at the World Cup. But it may be the most blatant example and stands as one of the darker moments in the tournament's history.

THE HAND OF GOD AND THE GOAL OF THE CENTURY

No single player has ever had a more memorable World Cup performance than Argentina's Diego Maradona did against England in 1986. In a span of four minutes, Maradona scored two of the most memorable goals in soccer history.

It all started in the 51st minute. Maradona controlled the ball and pressed toward the England goal. He kicked a diagonal pass in the direction of teammate Jorge Valdano. The pass came in a little behind Valdano, allowing England midfielder Steve Hodge to get a foot on it. Hodge's attempt to clear the ball failed, however. He knocked it high into the penalty area right in front of England's goal—and right back to Maradona. The forward reached out his hand and swatted

Diego Maradona (*left*) watches the ball sail into the goal after he smacked it with his hand. He would later say he didn't regret cheating to help his team beat England.

it past goalkeeper Peter Shilton. Because Maradona hit the ball with his hand, it was clear that the goal should be disallowed. Yet to everyone's surprise—including Maradona's—the referee signaled that the goal stood.

"I was waiting for my teammates to come embrace me, but no one came," Maradona said. "I told them, 'Come hug me, or the referee isn't going to allow it.'" After the game, Maradona described the play as, "a little with the head of Maradona and a little with the hand of God."

The Hand of God goal remains one of the most famous in World Cup history. Yet Maradona was just getting started. Four minutes after his bizarre goal, he took a pass near midfield. What followed was a one-man, 60-yard charge through the heart of England's defense. Maradona cut and weaved past defenders. He faked a shot that left Shilton on his back, then pounded the ball into the net to give Argentina a 2–0 lead. If Maradona's first goal left England feeling cheated, his second left them feeling helpless. The Goal of the Century, as it was called by fans, proved to be the difference in the game, and it forever etched Maradona's name into World Cup lore—this time, for the right reasons.

SCORE ONE FOR AFRICA
JUNE 8, 1990 • CAMEROON 1, ARGENTINA 0

It wasn't for the championship—it wasn't even an elimination match. In fact, it was the first match of that year's World Cup for both teams. That's not usually when the tournament gets turned upside down. Yet few matches in World Cup history have inspired the sort of legend that was born when Cameroon faced Argentina in the 1990 World Cup.

It was a mismatch of epic proportions. Argentina was at the top of the soccer world. They were the defending World Cup champions, with a roster filled with many of the game's biggest stars. Cameroon, which had enjoyed little success in international soccer, was composed of players who languished in the lower tiers of French leagues and some who hadn't even reached that level. African soccer as a whole was generally seen as second-rate—no African team had ever made a meaningful splash in the world's biggest tournament.

At least on paper, the match shouldn't have been close. Yet as the game dragged on, Cameroon's roster of largely overlooked players kept pace with the powerful Argentinians. What Cameroon lacked in technique, they made up for in physical play. Cameroon appeared to target Argentina's star forward, Diego Maradona, roughing him up at every opportunity.

The score remained 0–0 into the 61st minute. That's when Argentina's Claudio Caniggia took the ball on a free run toward Cameroon's goal. It was a golden opportunity, but Cameroon defender André Kana-Biyik broke it up with a vicious takedown. The move saved a goal but earned Kana-Biyik a red card, so he was ejected from the match and Cameroon would play the rest of the game down a man.

By any reasonable standard, that should have been a death blow for Cameroon's hopes. At even strength, their chances of beating Argentina seemed slim. With 10 players against Argentina's 11, it seemed almost impossible. Yet it was Cameroon taking the lead just minutes later on a deflected free kick. The crowd, strongly in the corner of the underdog, roared.

Just like that, Cameroon had a lead to protect. They stood in the way of a

Cameroon defenders (*in green*) swarmed around Diego Maradona whenever he touched the ball.

relentless Argentina attack, as goalkeeper Thomas N'Kono turned away chance after chance. The stadium grew louder and louder as the minutes ticked by. Regulation time neared an end. Then Caniggia broke free for Argentina. Cameroon defender Benjamin Massing slammed into Caniggia with a violent foul. Massing received a red card and was ejected for the play, but the score remained 1–0.

Playing 9 against 11 for the final minutes, Cameroon put up a frantic defensive effort, and time ran out on Argentina. It was a massive upset. Yet many fans were torn. They wanted to cheer on the underdogs, but Cameroon's rough play left many feeling uneasy about how they'd won.

Cameroon offered no apologies. Playing a rough, physical game was their only chance, and it had worked. And they didn't stop there. They went on to win their group, then advance all the way to the quarterfinals before losing to England, 3–2.

TAPPING IN A NEW ERA
NOVEMBER 30, 1991 • UNITED STATES 2, NORWAY 1

More than just a trophy was on the line at the first Women's World Cup in 1991. The tournament's success or failure would shape the future of women's soccer.

The final match featured Norway, which had bounced back after getting crushed in its opening contest with China, against the United States, a goal-scoring machine that had outscored its opponents 49–0 in pretournament qualifying matches.

Julie Foudy (*left*), Michelle Akers-Stahl (*center*), and Carin Jennings celebrate with the 1991 Women's World Cup trophy.

About 60,000 fans packed Tianhe Stadium in Guangzhou, China, to watch the teams battle for the championship.

If the United States had expected a cakewalk, they were in for a rude awakening. After an evenly played first half ended 1–1, Norway controlled much of the second-half action. Yet with just two minutes remaining in regulation time, it was the United States on the attack. Star forward Michelle Akers-Stahl intercepted a pass deep in Norway's end. Akers-Stahl was all alone. Norway's goalkeeper, Reidun Seth, came out to challenge. But Akers-Stahl calmly tapped the ball behind Seth. Only six yards of open grass stood between the US forward and the goal.

Akers-Stahl sized up her shot. "Everyone told me afterwards their hearts were stopping because they didn't think I would ever shoot the ball," she said.

But she did shoot, a tap that sent the ball rolling over the line to put the United States in the lead for good. It was the first international soccer championship for any US team, and it marked the birth of a true international powerhouse.

Mia Hamm was used to scoring goals, not stopping them. She retired from the US national team in 2004 with 158 goals, the most of any player at the time.

MIA DOES IT ALL

JUNE 8, 1995 • UNITED STATES 2, DENMARK 0

A mostly unremarkable game became an incredible story at the 1995 Women's World Cup when a scoring hero stepped in to save the day. The United States was on its way to a comfortable victory over Denmark.

Then, with about six minutes remaining, things got strange. Officials gave US goalkeeper Briana Scurry a controversial red card, meaning that she was disqualified from the rest of the game.

The United States had already used all three of its allowed substitutions. That meant the team didn't have a goalkeeper. In stepped forward Mia Hamm. Hamm was a goal-scoring phenomenon and one of the biggest stars in women's soccer.

As the crowd chanted her name, Hamm proved that she could do it all. She stopped several shots from Denmark to preserve the shutout and give the United States the victory. Most of the game was forgettable. But no one who saw it would ever forget seeing one of the world's most dangerous goal scorers transform into a goalkeeper.

THE PERFECT GOAL
JULY 4, 1998 • NETHERLANDS 2, ARGENTINA 1

World Cup fans can argue endlessly about the greatest goal ever scored. But one thing is certain. No matter who is arguing or where they're from, Dennis Bergkamp's amazing goal in the 1998 quarterfinals is always on the short list.

Argentina and the Netherlands were engaged in a 1–1 deadlock as the final seconds of regulation time ticked away. Frank de Boer of the Netherlands booted a towering 70-yard pass down the field, toward a streaking Bergkamp. The ball was out in front of Bergkamp, but he timed a leap perfectly and brought the ball under control with his right foot.

"I didn't realize how high in the air I was," Bergkamp said of his remarkable leap. "But you know you want that ball in that position. . . . So you have to jump up to meet the ball."

A defender cut in front of Bergkamp to end the charge. But in one seamless motion, the Dutch forward dribbled the ball behind the defender, changed his momentum, and sent the defender past him. Without a moment of hesitation, the athletic forward unleashed a shot to the upper-left corner of the goal, blasting it past Argentina's goalkeeper.

The two seconds of perfection sent the Netherlands to the semifinals. "You're in that moment," Bergkamp said. "That's the feeling. After the first two touches, that moment! You give absolutely everything. It's like your life has led up to this moment. . . . You never play the perfect game. But the moment itself was, I think, perfect."

Dennis Bergkamp (*left*) keeps his eye on the ball just before scoring against Argentina. *The Guardian* newspaper later called it a "wonder goal."

CHASTAIN'S GOLDEN GOAL
JULY 10, 1999 • UNITED STATES 0 (5), CHINA 0 (4)

The Women's World Cup was just eight years old when the United States hosted it in 1999. But already, it had grown beyond FIFA's wildest dreams. While the men's game in the United States still lagged behind the rest of the world, the women's game was thriving.

The US women rolled through group play before winning tight matches over Germany and Brazil to advance to the championship game. With heavy media coverage of the event, the team's run captured the imagination of many US fans—even those who had never before seen a women's match. The team's stars, from goalkeeper Briana Scurry to forward Mia Hamm, were household names.

The US women faced China for the World Cup title. Many fans came expecting a shootout. Instead, they got a defensive clash. For 90 minutes, the two teams engaged in a tense but scoreless chess match. Another 30 minutes of extra time left the score 0–0. That meant it all came down to penalty kicks. Each team would get five tries.

The penalty kick strongly favors the offensive player. The goalkeeper is often forced to guess which direction the ball will go. The first two kickers for each team scored. In the third round, China's Liu Ying approached the ball. As she did, Scurry inched out of the goal and then dove to her left. It was the right move. Scurry batted the ball away, denying China. Kristine Lilly banged her kick in to give the United States a lead, 3–2. The crowd was on its feet, a roaring sea of red, white, and blue.

Both teams scored in the fourth round, and China added a goal in the fifth. That left it all up to the final US kicker, defender Brandi Chastain, who had missed a penalty kick against China just three months earlier. Most soccer players have a preferred foot for kicking the ball. But Chastain was a true two-footed player, equally dangerous with the left and the right. This time, she went to the left, quickly approaching and booting the ball toward the right corner of China's goal. Goalkeeper Gao Hong dove for it, but the ball whizzed past her outstretched fingers. Goal! The United States had won the shootout, 5–4. The stadium

Brandi Chastain's goal celebration was one of the most memorable moments of the 1999 Women's World Cup.

erupted as Chastain ripped off her white jersey and dropped to her knees as her teammates sprinted across the field to mob her.

Chastain later explained her famous celebration. "It was a combination of things: joy, relief, satisfaction, the desire to do well for your team, your country, your family. Those are emotions that you carry around every day for years and finally I could let it all out."

It was a game and a tournament that captured the imaginations of sports fans in the United States and around the world. No game, no goal, and no celebration has done more to elevate women's soccer.

A SHOCKING EXIT
JULY 9, 2006 • ITALY 1 (5), FRANCE 1 (3)

The 2006 World Cup championship match was a classic struggle between France and Italy. The game was filled with precision passing, stout defense, and a thrilling finish. Yet it was the actions of one player—France's Zinedine Zidane—that left a lasting memory.

Zidane had already announced that he was playing the final match of an incredible career—he was widely seen as one of the greatest players in the history of Europe. He was looking to cement his legacy by leading France to a World Cup title. Instead, Zidane cemented a legacy of a very different kind.

The game was even at 1–1 in extra time. France was on the attack. Zidane connected on a header that almost put France in the lead, but goalkeeper Gianluigi Buffon made a game-saving stop.

As Zidane was jogging back toward midfield, he exchanged words with Italy's Marco Materazzi. Exactly what was said remains a matter of debate. But what happened next is not. Zidane started to walk away from Materazzi. Then he abruptly turned around and slammed his head into the Italian's chest, sending Materazzi sprawling to the ground.

Zinedine Zidane (*left*) knocks Marco Materazzi to the turf. Zidane continued playing in charity matches and was named manager of Spain's popular Real Madrid team in 2016.

It was a shockingly violent act. Officials gave Zidanc a red card and expelled him from the game. He could only watch helplessly as his teammates lost on penalty kicks and Italy celebrated the championship. His career was over, and his head butt remains the lasting image of one of the game's greats.

Zidane was vilified for his act, both in France and internationally. He later apologized, saying, "This isn't justification, this isn't an excuse, but my passion, temper, and blood made me react."

JAPAN ARRIVES
JULY 17, 2011 • JAPAN 2 (3), USA 2 (1)

Entering the 2011 women's tournament, the world's most populous continent, Asia, was still without a title in men's or women's World Cup play. And there was little reason to believe that would change anytime soon. Asia's best team that year, Japan, had never even reached the semifinals of a World Cup.

Japan was out to change that. After shocking the host nation, Germany, in the quarterfinals, Japan beat Sweden in the semifinals to reach the championship match against the powerhouse of women's soccer, the top-ranked United States.

The Americans were heavy favorites. The United States and Japan had played each other 25 times before, and the United States had never lost. The US women were the more athletic team, known for a relentless attacking style. Yet every time the Americans took control of the match, Japan was there to answer back. US forward Alex Morgan struck first with a goal in the 69th minute, and Japan's Aya Miyama responded with a score just 10 minutes later.

The United States again seized control during extra time when superstar Abby Wambach knocked in a go-ahead header in the 104th minute. Japan staged a frantic charge as the clock ticked away. With just three minutes remaining, Japan's Homare Sawa fired at the net. Goalkeeper Hope Solo was ready for the shot. But as Solo moved to make the stop, the ball deflected off Wambach, changing its direction.

Homare Sawa (*in blue*) takes a shot with her back to the goal. The ball sailed through a gang of US defenders and into the net.

Solo had no chance. The ball crossed the goal line, and Japan celebrated the stunning score.

It was on to penalty kicks. The United States' first three kickers, all of whom were accomplished in taking such kicks, missed their attempts before Wambach converted the fourth. Japan, meanwhile, converted on two of its first three tries. That gave Japan's Saki Kumagai a shot to win it with Japan's fourth try. Kumagai blasted her shot to the left. Solo dove for it, but the ball sailed past her fingertips and into the back of the net. Japan stormed the field in celebration. It was one of the biggest upsets in Women's World Cup history and officially put Japan on the map as one of the powers of the sport.

A CLASSIC IN RIO
JULY 13, 2014 • GERMANY 1, ARGENTINA 0

The 2014 World Cup gave Brazil a chance to warm up for the 2016 Olympic Games, to be held in Rio de Janeiro, Brazil. And while Brazilian fans were disappointed that their green-and-gold team didn't make the final World Cup match, they were treated to a defensive classic between Germany and Argentina for the title.

Germany was widely regarded as the team to beat at the 2014 World Cup, while Argentina was led by Lionel Messi—the world's best player, according to many fans and commentators. It was a tense, defensive struggle. Argentina appeared to take a lead in the first half on a goal by Gonzalo Higuaín, but the referee ruled him offside and disallowed the goal.

The 0–0 deadlock dragged on into the second half, with both teams clamping down on defense. Germany's Benedikt Höwedes nearly gave his team the lead with a header, but the shot just missed, bouncing off the crossbar instead. After 90 minutes, the match remained scoreless. It was on to 30 minutes of extra time.

Lionel Messi (*right*) is one of soccer's all-time great goal scorers, but he couldn't put one past the German defense at the 2014 World Cup.

The tension grew and grew. In the 113th minute, Germany controlled the ball on a rush inside the Argentina end. André Schürrle sent a crossing pass ahead, where midfielder Mario Götze had gotten behind the Argentina defense. The pass came in high, but Götze managed to bring it down with his chest. In one fluid motion, Götze slid, sending a left-footed volley past the goalkeeper. Germany mobbed him in front of the goal. After the celebration, the German team held on for the last seven minutes to claim the title.

HEARTBREAK

JULY 1, 2015 • JAPAN 2, ENGLAND 1

Heartbreak is no stranger at the World Cup. However, few teams have experienced it quite like England did at the 2015 Women's World Cup. As they squared off with Japan in the semifinal round, England was looking to reach the tournament's final match for the first time. It was no easy task. Japan was the defending champion, with a precision passing attack second to none.

The score was knotted, 1–1, as the 90th minute passed. With only a minute or two of injury time remaining, the match appeared to be headed to extra time. Japan controlled the ball on England's side of the pitch. Japan's Nahomi Kawasumi sent a deep pass in front of England's goal. One of her teammates was streaking toward the net, but the pass came in behind her.

England's Laura Bassett slid to clear the ball away from the front of the goal. Bassett was trying to boot it safely out of the area. But that's not what happened. Bassett's clearing attempt sailed high toward the upper-right corner of the goal and banged off the crossbar, over the head of goalkeeper Karen Bardsley. Bassett, lying prone on the grass, could only watch in horror as her failed clearing attempt fell down beyond the goal line. She had accidentally scored on her own goal. Just like that, Japan was ahead, 2–1. The final whistle blew moments later, leaving England stunned and Bassett in tears.

Laura Bassett (*background, center*) puts her hands on her knees after scoring on her own goal. She would later say that support from fans and teammates helped her get through the worst moment of her soccer career.

WORLD CUP CHAMPIONS

MEN'S WORLD CUP

Year	Winner	Runner-Up	Score
1930	Uruguay	Argentina	4–2
1934	Italy	Czechoslovakia	2–1
1938	Italy	Hungary	4–2
1950	Uruguay	Brazil	2–1
1954	West Germany	Hungary	3–2
1958	Brazil	Sweden	5–2
1962	Brazil	Czechoslovakia	3–1
1966	England	West Germany	4–2
1970	Brazil	Italy	4–1
1974	West Germany	Netherlands	2–1
1978	Argentina	Netherlands	3–1
1982	Italy	West Germany	3–1
1986	Argentina	West Germany	3–2
1990	West Germany	Argentina	1–0
1994	Brazil	Italy	0–0 (3–2)
1998	France	Brazil	3–0
2002	Brazil	Germany	2–0
2006	Italy	France	1–1 (5–3)
2010	Spain	Netherlands	1–0
2014	Germany	Argentina	1–0

WOMEN'S WORLD CUP

Year	Winner	Runner-Up	Score
1991	USA	Norway	2–1
1995	Norway	Germany	2–0
1999	USA	China	0–0 (5–4)
2003	Germany	Sweden	2–1
2007	Germany	Brazil	2–0
2011	Japan	USA	2–2 (3–1)
2015	USA	Japan	5–2

3 A WORLDWIDE CELEBRATION:
THE CULTURE OF THE WORLD CUP

The World Cup has grown into one of the biggest international sporting events in the world, nurturing a following almost on par with the Olympic Games. As fans from all over the globe gather to watch soccer, they blend to form a unique group that transcends class, race, economic background, and language.

MELTING POT

While players in the World Cup stay in luxury hotels—often battling boredom between practices and matches—there is plenty to keep fans entertained. The World Cup welcomes all cultures. Fans from very different backgrounds gather by the hundreds of thousands, mixing and meeting on common ground: their love of the game. The tournament moves around the globe, giving fans the chance to soak up new experiences and new traditions as they cheer on their teams.

The action on the pitch is the main draw, but the tournament stretches on for weeks, leaving fans with plenty of free time. The areas immediately around the stadiums are usually the centers of activity. Many fans enjoy taking in the culture of the host country. They sample popular food, visit tourist attractions, shop for souvenirs, and meet the local people. Many flock to fan parties, where they wear their teams' colors and wave their nations' flags.

Much like the Olympics, the World Cup kicks off with a star-studded opening ceremony. The stadium is packed as dancers and singers take to the stage. In 2014 Brazil welcomed superstar musicians including Jennifer Lopez, Pitbull, and Claudia Leitte for the ceremony. Four years before that, Shakira electrified the crowd with a stirring performance of "Waka Waka (This Time for Africa)," setting the mood for the excitement to follow.

Pitbull (*left*), Claudia Leitte (*center*), and Jennifer Lopez perform together at the 2014 World Cup.

The party atmosphere really kicks into high gear when the host country posts a victory. In 2014, whenever Brazil won a match, the celebration spilled into the streets. Locals and foreign fans alike danced as funk and samba music filled the air. A heavy police presence helped to ensure that the partying didn't get out of hand.

Even fans of a losing team get in on the act. When a nation's team is eliminated, a small portion of fans respond with tears or violent outbursts. But most of them decide instead to root for a team still in the hunt, such as an underdog, the host nation, or a team playing against their biggest rival.

No matter who wins on the pitch, World Cup fans have a great time in the stands.

HOOLIGANISM

Poorly behaved fans have long been a problem for big soccer events. Often called hooligans, these fans engage in violent and unruly behavior. That can range from verbal abuse to vandalism to outright brawling.

Hooliganism is most commonly tied to league soccer, mainly in European nations. However, it has also made its way onto the international stage. In 2014 Brazilian hooligans attacked English fans, and security guards also dealt with problems such as fans breaking through a gate outside the stadium (*below*). Russian hooligans plagued a 2016 international tournament, giving rise to fears that they could repeat the act at the 2018 World Cup.

World Cup organizers have taken measures to reduce hooliganism. They have banned items that could be used as weapons. They do their best to keep the fan bases for each side on opposite ends of a stadium to reduce the chances of fighting. And they deny stadium access to anyone who is a known hooligan. Meanwhile, an increased police presence in and around the stadium helps to keep bad behavior to a minimum. Yet hooliganism remains a real problem. For some fans, the world's biggest soccer tournament is little more than an excuse to create trouble and mayhem, putting a damper on the spirit of international competition all around them.

INSIDE THE STADIUM

The tension ramps up as the start of the match approaches. Fans fill the stadium, dressed in their nation's colors. Security and police forces are always present but rarely needed.

After a coin toss decides which team will kick off, the match begins. The atmosphere is electric. The crowd roars and often remains standing for much of or all the match. Fans wave banners in support of their favorite teams or players. Some paint their faces or dress in wild costumes.

The flavor of every World Cup is different, and it's hard to know just what will capture the imagination of the fans. The 2010 tournament became famous for the vuvuzela, a long trumpetlike instrument that gives a signature buzzing sound. The wail of the vuvuzelas in the stadiums was so loud and so constant that some onlookers started to worry about hearing loss. Yet most of those in attendance seemed unconcerned, happily wailing away on the instrument and often passing them from person to person around the stadium. The vuvuzela craze briefly spread, with the instruments showing up at other sporting events around the world.

Watch any big World Cup match and one of the things you'll notice is the fan chants. The rhythmic phrases can thunder through the stadium

A fan of South Africa's national team blows a vuvuzela at the 2010 World Cup. The first vuvuzelas were made of metal, and they began showing up at sporting events in the 1990s.

as fans of different teams try to outshout one another. Almost every nation's fan base has its own unique sets of chants, and they come in every language the World Cup has to offer.

Brazil fans sing and chant at a match during the 2014 World Cup.

Most chants are short phrases shouted to encourage a team. Fans of the United States often go with the simple yet distinct "U-S-A! U-S-A!" Chile's fans shout *Chi-chi-chi Le-le-le!* French fans cheer on their blue-clad team with the chant, *Allez Les Bleus*, which is French for *Go Blue!* Argentina celebrates the legendary Lionel Messi with their chant, *Ole, ole, ole. Messi, Messi!* Japanese fans, meanwhile, borrow the Spanish word *vamos* for their chant, *Vamos Nippon* (Let's Go Japan).

Not all the fan chants are so friendly, however. Fans also use chants to mock or taunt the opposing team. In 2014 England and Germany met in the World Cup. England's fans adapted the tune from the song "Camptown Races" with the lyrics, "Two World Wars and one World Cup, England, England. Two World Wars and one World Cup, England all the way." The song was a jab at Germans for having been on the losing side of two world wars, as well as the 1966 World Cup. Meanwhile, Mexican fans have drawn criticism for a vulgar one-word chant shouted at any opposing goalkeeper who allows a goal.

The encouraging chants tend to drown out the mean-spirited ones, though, and chanting remains a unique and memorable part of the World Cup fan experience.

FOCUS ON THE GAME

In many ways, the World Cup lacks much of the pomp of other major sporting events. The World Cup, unlike the Super Bowl, is not taken over by corporate guests who pay outrageous ticket prices to attend games. Many individual World Cup match tickets are priced so that fans don't have to pay thousands of dollars to go—tickets are often less than $100. Even at the final match, with tens of millions of fans watching on television, halftime is limited to 15 minutes—the same as any

Members of Germany's national team celebrate their World Cup title in 2014.

POLITICS ASIDE

One of the greatest aspects of the World Cup is the international goodwill the competition creates. No matter the politics between two nations, they set aside their differences to enjoy the world's most popular sport together.

That was never more evident than in 1998 when the United States and Iran met in France. Political relations between the nations had been tense for decades. French officials assigned extra security at the game, fearing violent outbursts.

They had no reason to worry. The fans shared the stadium without incident, and the play on the field was the picture of sportsmanship. Before the game, the team captains exchanged gifts at the center circle, and the teams posed together for photographs.

Iran won the match, 2–1. But the final score was secondary to the message the players and fans sent to the world. For at least one moment, a game allowed two nations to set their differences aside and let soccer and sportsmanship rule the day.

other international match. There is no fancy halftime show. Instead, groundskeepers spend those 15 minutes repairing the field. The focus remains on soccer, rather than the sideshows. Halftime is when fans use the restrooms and concession stands. When the players return to the pitch, it's right back to business.

After the final whistle sounds, the winners celebrate on the field. There, they are presented with the golden World Cup trophy as their fans cheer. And just like that, it's over. Over the next few days, the fans and players return home. The party dies down. Life returns to normal. The World Cup is over, but the preparation is only beginning for the next host country.

4 THE FUTURE
OF THE WORLD CUP

The world's biggest soccer tournament has come a long way since it debuted in 1930. The World Cup helped to usher in an era of international soccer that has swept over the world. What does the future hold?

The World Cup's popularity has been growing for generations, and it shows no signs of slowing anytime soon. In 2017 FIFA announced a plan to expand the men's tournament from 32 teams to 48 by 2026 (the Women's World Cup expanded from 16 teams to 24 in 2015). FIFA officials argued that expansion would allow more teams from more regions to compete, generate more money, and help grow the sport.

"We are in the 21st century, and we have to shape the football World Cup of the 21st century," said Gianni Infantino, the president of FIFA. "Football is more than just Europe and South America. Football is global."

The move came with criticism, however. Some fans argued that expansion would water down the quality of the matches. And the proposed format would send 16 of the teams home after losing just a single match.

Yet including more countries promises to help ignite interest in places where soccer's popularity still lags, including in North America. Soccer in the United States and Canada is on the rise, especially among youth. Professional leagues such

Fans watch the final match of the 2014 World Cup in the courtyard of the National Portrait Gallery and Smithsonian American Art Museum in Washington, DC. The event was free for soccer fans of all ages.

as Major League Soccer (MLS) are expanding, helping to grow a larger and more knowledgeable fan base.

Meanwhile, FIFA wants to use the World Cup as the centerpiece of its plan to promote soccer worldwide. Its goals include expanding the sport in the world's poorest nations and increasing participation among women.

International soccer is much different than it was when the World Cup debuted in 1930. But much remains the same. After eight decades of play, only two continents—Europe and South America—have ever boasted a men's World Cup winner. When will that change? And what will it mean for the sport when new powers arise? Soccer fans can't wait to find out.

SOURCE NOTES

10 "A Historical Link with the Franche-Comté," FIFA, June 17, 1998, http://www.fifa.com/news/y=1998 /m=6/news=historical-link-with-the-franche-comte-71490.html.

19 Barbara Basler, "Soccer; U.S. Women Beat Norway to Capture World Cup," *New York Times*, December 1, 1991, http://www.nytimes.com/1991/12/01/sports/soccer-us-women-beat-norway-to-capture-world -cup.html.

26 Scott Murray, "World Cup: 25 Stunning Moments . . . No2: Uruguay's 1950 Triumph in Brazil," *Guardian* (US ed.), February 18, 2014, https://www.theguardian.com/football/blog/2014/feb/18/world -cup-25-stunning-moments-no2-uruguay-brazil-1950-scott-murray.

28 John Ashdown, "World Cup: 25 Stunning Moments . . . No14: the Miracle of Bern," *Guardian* (US ed.), May 6, 2014, https://www.theguardian.com/football/blog/2014/may/06/world-cup-stunning-moments -miracle-of-bern.

29 Ibid.

30 "Brilliant Banks Denies Pele Header," FIFA, October 13, 2016, http://www.fifa.com/worldcup/news /y=2016/m=10/news=brilliant-banks-denies-pele-header-2842873.html.

33 Rob Smyth, "World Cup: 25 Stunning Moments . . . No3: West Germany 1–0 Austria in 1982," *Guardian* (US ed.), February 25, 2014, https://www.theguardian.com/football/blog/2014/feb/25/world -cup-25-stunning-moments-no3-germany-austria-1982-rob-smyth.

35 "Argentina's World Cup Quarter-Final against England in Mexico in 1986 Became One of the Most Famous Games in Football History Thanks to One Man," *Goal*, April 13, 2017, http://www.goal.com /en-us/news/67/world-cup/2017/04/13/34579392/diego-maradona-the-hand-of-god-the-most-infamous -goal-in.

38 Phil Hersh, "U.S. Women Win World Soccer Title," *Chicago Tribune*, December 1, 1991, http://articles .chicagotribune.com/1991-12-01/sports/9104180653_1_norwegian-defender-tina-svensson-world-soccer -title-michelle-akers-stahl.

39 "1998 Holland-Argentina: Bergkamp's 'Perfect' Goal," *Hindu*, July 7, 2014, http://www.thehindu.com /sport/football/fifa-2014/1998-hollandargentina-bergkamps-perfect-goal/article6185265.ece.

40 Ibid.

42 Ben Lyttleton, "Brandi Chastain on 1999 Penalty: 'All Your Hopes and Fears in One Moment,'" *Guardian* (US ed.), June 30, 2015, https://www.theguardian.com/football/2015/jun/30/brandi-chastain-penalty-all -fears-hopes.

43 Matt Pomroy, "Zinedine Zidane," *Esquire*, August 4, 2015, http://www.esquireme.com/culture/zinedine -zidane.

58 Andrew Keh, "FIFA to Expand World Cup to 48 Teams in 2026," *New York Times*, January 10, 2017, https://www.nytimes.com/2017/01/10/sports/fifa-world-cup.html.

GLOSSARY

crossing pass: a pass that crosses the field in front of the goal

dribble: to control the ball with short kicks

extra time: 30 minutes of time added to games after regulation time and injury time have ended

forward: a soccer position that is responsible for scoring goals

free kick: a kick awarded to a team after the other team has committed a foul. A free kick is an unchallenged kick to resume play.

hat trick: when a single player scores three goals in a match

injury time: time added after the end of regulation time to make up for stoppages in play for injuries or other reasons

midfielder: a soccer position that usually plays between a team's forwards and defenders

offside: illegally ahead of the ball on the other team's side of the field

penalty kick: a free kick at the goal from about 12 yards away, awarded by the referee after a foul near the goal

pitch: a soccer field

red card: a card held by the referee to indicate a player has broken a rule and will be ejected from the match

round-robin: a format in which each team in a group plays every other team in that group

FURTHER READING

Beginner's Guide to Soccer
http://ussoccerplayers.com/beginners-guide-to-soccer

FIFA World Cup: Russia 2018
http://www.fifa.com/worldcup

Jökulsson, Illugi. *Stars of the World Cup*. New York: Abbeville Kids, 2014.

———. *U.S. Women's Team: Soccer Champions!* New York: Abbeville, 2015.

Kennedy, Mike, and Mark Stewart. *Goal! The Fire and Fury of Soccer's Greatest Moment*. Minneapolis: Millbrook Press, 2010.

Morgan, Alex. *Breakaway: Beyond the Goal*. New York: Simon & Schuster, 2015.

Trusdell, Brian. *Pelé: Soccer Star & Ambassador*. Minneapolis: ABDO, 2014.

———. *US Women Win the World Cup*. Minneapolis: SportsZone, 2015.

U.S. Soccer
https://www.ussoccer.com

US Youth Soccer
http://www.usyouthsoccer.org

INDEX

ABOUT THE AUTHOR

Matt Doeden began his career as a sportswriter. Since then he's spent more than a decade writing and editing more than 100 children's nonfiction books. His books *The Super Bowl: Chasing Football Immortality*, *The Negro Leagues: Celebrating Baseball's Unsung Heroes*, *The World Series: Baseball's Biggest Stage*, *Sandy Koufax*, and *Tom Brady: Unlikely Champion* were Junior Library Guild selections. Doeden lives in Minnesota with his wife and two children.

PHOTO ACKNOWLEDGMENTS

The images in this book are used with the permission of: MIS/PIXATHLON/Newscom, p. 4; Hulton Archive/Getty Images, p. 6; Bob Thomas/Popperfoto/Getty Images, pp. 9, 12, 25; PA Images/Alamy Stock Photo, pp. 10, 28; EMPICS/Newscom, p. 11; A.RICARDO/Shutterstock.com, p. 14; Popperfoto/Getty Images, pp. 16, 26, 30; FOTOSPORTS INTERNATIONAL/Newscom, p. 17; Bob Thomas/Getty Images, pp. 18, 34; TOMMY CHENG/AFP/Getty Images, pp. 19, 37; MIKE BLAKE/REUTERS/Newscom, p. 20; 360b/Shutterstock.com, p. 21; Jefferson Bernardes/Shutterstock.com, pp. 22, 46, 56; Ferdi Hartung/ullstein bild/Getty Images, p. 31; AP Photo/Mönckebild, p. 33; Ross Kinnaird/EMPICS/Getty Images, p. 36; George Tiedemann/Sports Illustrated/Getty Images, p. 38; Michael Steele/EMPICS/Getty Images, p. 40; ROBERTO SCHMIDT/AFP/Getty Images, p. 41; JOHN MACDOUGALL/AFP/Getty Images, p. 43; sampics/Corbis/Getty Images, p. 44; Vaughn Ridley/ZUMA Press/Newscom, p. 47; AGIF/Shutterstock.com, p. 51; CP DC Press/Shutterstock.com, p. 52; Julian Finney/Getty Images, p. 53; fstockfoto/Shutterstock.com, p. 54; Dennis Grombkowski/FIFA/Getty Images, p. 55; Kate Patterson/The Washington Post/Getty Images, p. 59. Design elements: iStock.com/idimair; iStock.com/GeorgePeters; iStock.com/MichaelJay; iStock.com/sumnersgraphicsinc.

Front cover: Fotoarena/Sipa USA/Newscom (World Cup 2014), iStock.com/idimair (background). Flap: sampics/Corbis/Getty Images.